...tré em gái   Santuario per le ragazze   ضريح للفتيات   Scrín do chailíní   女孩的神殿   Svatyně pro dívky   लड़कियों के
מקדש עבור ב...   Храм за момичета   Sanctuaire pour les filles   여자에 대 한 신...   Kuil un...

D0618338

लड़कियों के लिए तीर्थ   Santuário para meninas   Храм для девочек   Shrine for G...   ...n für Mäd...
Kuil untuk anak perempuan   Miếu thờ cho trẻ em gái   Santuario per le ragaz...   ...자에 대 한   女
...n für Mädchen   Santuario de las niñas   מקדש עבור בנות   Храм за момичет...   ...자에 대 한
...hailíní   女孩的神殿   Svatyně pro dívky   लड़कियों के लिए तीर्थ   Santuário para meninas   Храм для девочек   Shrine for
...대 한 신사   Παρεκκλήσι για τα κορίτσια   Kuil untuk anak perempuan   Miếu thờ cho trẻ em gái   Santuario per le rag...
Shrine for Girls   女の子のための神社   Schrein für Mädchen   Santuario de las niñas   מקדש עבור בנות   Храм за моми...
...io per le ragazze   ضريح للفتيات   Scrín do chailíní   女孩的神殿   Svatyně pro dívky   लड़कियों के लिए तीर्थ   Santuário
...ам за момичета   Sanctuaire pour les filles   여자에 대 한 신사   Παρεκκλήσι για τα κορίτσια   Kuil untuk anak peremp...
Santuário para meninas   Храм для девочек   Shrine for Girls   女の子のための神社   Schrein für Mädchen   Santuario d...
...perempuan   Miếu thờ cho trẻ em gái   Santuario per le ragazze   ضريح للفتيات   Scrín do chailíní   女孩的神殿   Sva...
...antuario de las niñas   מקדש עבור בנות   Храм за момичета   Sanctuaire pour les filles   여자에 대 한 신사   Παρεκκλήσι
殿   Svatyně pro dívky   लड़कियों के लिए तीर्थ   Santuário para meninas   Храм для девочек   Shrine for Girls   女の子のた...
...ρεκκλήσι για τα κορίτσια   Kuil untuk anak perempuan   Miếu thờ cho trẻ em gái   Santuario per le ragazze   ح للفتيات
...子のための神社   Schrein für Mädchen   Santuario de las niñas   מקדש עבור בנות   Храм за момичета   Sanctuaire pou...
...ية ضريح للفتيات   Scrín do chailíní   女孩的神殿   Svatyně pro dívky   लड़कियों के लिए तीर्थ   Santuário para meninas   Храм
...ctuaire pour les filles   여자에 대 한 신사   Παρεκκλήσι για τα κορίτσια   Kuil untuk anak perempuan   Miếu thờ cho trẻ
...as   Храм для девочек   Shrine for Girls   女の子のための神社   Schrein für Mädchen   Santuario de las niñas   עבור בנות
...ờ trẻ em gái   Santuario per le ragazze   ضريح للفتيات   Scrín do chailíní   女孩的神殿   Svatyně pro dívky   लड़कियों के
מקדש עבור בנ...   Храм за момичета   Sanctuaire pour les filles   여자에 대 한 신사   Παρεκκλήσι για τα κορίτσια   Kuil u
लड़कियों के लिए तीर्थ   Santuário para meninas   Храм для девочек   Shrine for Girls   女の子のための神社   Schrein für Mäde...
Kuil untuk anak perempuan   Miếu thờ cho trẻ em gái   Santuario per le ragazze   ضريح للفتيات   Scrín do chailíní   女
...n für Mädchen   Santuario de las niñas   מקדש עבור בנות   Храм за момичета   Sanctuaire pour les filles   여자에 대 한
...hailíní   女孩的神殿   Svatyně pro dívky   लड़कियों के लिए तीर्थ   Santuário para meninas   Храм для девочек   Shrine for
...에 대 한 신사   Παρεκκλήσι για τα κορίτσια   Kuil untuk anak perempuan   Miếu thờ cho trẻ em gái   Santuario per le rag...
Shrine for Girls   女の子のための神社   Schrein für Mädchen   Santuario de las niñas   מקדש עבור בנות   Храм за моми...
...io per le ragazze   ضريح للفتيات   Scrín do chailíní   女孩的神殿   Svatyně pro dívky   लड़कियों के लिए तीर्थ   Santuário
...ам за момичета   Sanctuaire pour les filles   여자에 대 한 신사   Παρεκκλήσι για τα κορίτσια   Kuil untuk anak peremp...
Santuário para meninas   Храм для девочек   Shrine for Girls   女の子のための神社   Schrein für Mädchen   Santuario d...
...k perempuan   Miếu thờ cho trẻ em gái   Santuario per le ragazze   ضريح للفتيات   Scrín do chailíní   女孩的神殿   Sva...
...antuario de las niñas   מקדש עבור בנות   Храм за момичета   Sanctuaire pour les filles   여자에 대 한 신사   Παρεκκλήσι
神殿   Svatyně pro dívky   लड़कियों के लिए तीर्थ   Santuário para meninas   Храм для девочек   Shrine for Girls   女の子のた
...ρεκκλήσι για τα κορίτσια   Kuil untuk anak perempuan   Miếu thờ cho trẻ em gái   Santuario per le ragazze   ح للفتيات
...子のための神社   Schrein für Mädchen   Santuario de las niñas   מקדש עבור בנות   Храм за момичета   Sanctuaire pou...
...ية ضريح للفتيات   Scrín do chailíní   女孩的神殿   Svatyně pro dívky   लड़कियों के लिए तीर्थ   Santuário para meninas   Храм
...ctuaire pour les filles   여자에 대 한 신사   Παρεκκλήσι για τα κορίτσια   Kuil untuk anak perempuan   Miếu thờ cho trẻ

Shrine for Girls

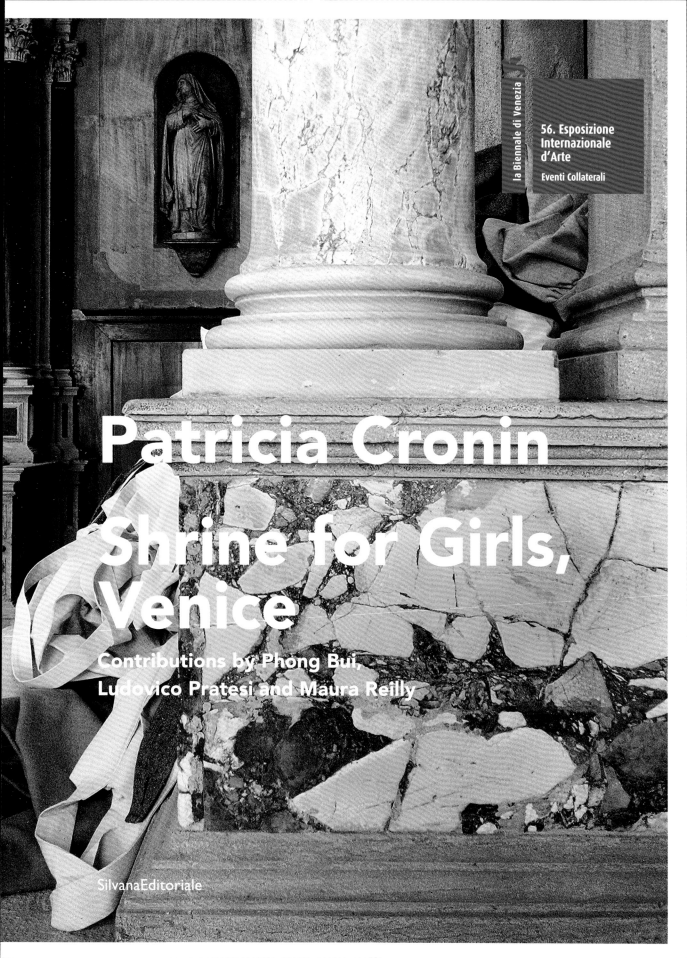

la Biennale di Venezia

56. Esposizione Internazionale d'Arte
Eventi Collaterali

Patricia Cronin

Shrine for Girls, Venice

Contributions by Phong Bui, Ludovico Pratesi and Maura Reilly

SilvanaEditoriale

Shrine For Girls, Venice

Published on the occasion of the exhibition
Shrine For Girls, Venice, a solo Collateral
Event of the 56th International Art Exhibition -
la Biennale di Venezia 2015.

Shrine For Girls, Venice
May 9–November 22, 2015
Chiesa di San Gallo, Campo San Gallo,
Venice, Italy

Curated by Ludovico Pratesi

Presented by Brooklyn Rail Curatorial Projects

THE BROOKLYN RAIL

Lead Sponsors

The **FLAG** Art Foundation

The Fuhrman Family Foundation

Art Director
Beverly Joel, pulp, ink.

Typesetting and layout
pulp, ink.

Photo Credits
Cover and pages 2–3, 12–13, 20–21, 23, 24–25, 27, 28–29,
31–35, 64: Mark Blower
Page 5: Vincent Wai Him Hui
Pages 10, 16: Beverly Joel
Page 39: Musees Royaux des Beaux-Arts de Belgique,
Brussels, BelgiumMondadori Portfolio/Electa/Sergio Anelli/
Bridgeman Images
Page 40: © Isabella Stewart Gardner Museum,
Boston, MA, USA/Bridgeman Images
Page 43: Courtesy Patricia Cronin, and Collection
Petit Palais, Paris, Courtesy of Wiki Commons
Page 44: Courtesy Patricia Cronin
Page 46: Collection Mrs. Eric de Spoelberch,
Haverford, PA, Courtesy of Wiki Commons
Pages 49–55: Nicholas Knight

Cover
Installation view of *Shrine for Girls, Venice*, 2015

www.shrineforgirls.org

SilvanaEditoriale

Direction
Dario Cimorelli

Art Director
Giacomo Merli

Production Coordinator
Michela Bramati

Editorial Assistant
Ondina Granato

Photo Editor
Alessandra Olivari, Silvia Sala

Press Office
Lidia Masolini, press@silvanaeditoriale.it

All reproduction and translation
rights reserved for all countries
© 2015 Silvana Editoriale S.p.A.,
Cinisello Balsamo, Milano

Silvana Editoriale S.p.A.
via dei Lavoratori, 78
20092 Cinisello Balsamo, Milano
tel. +39 02 453 951 01
fax +39 02 453 951 51
www.silvanaeditoriale.it

ISBN 9788836632190

Reproductions, printing and binding in Italy
Printed by Grafiche Aurora, Verona
Printed August 2015

Foreword

Phong Bui

"**The human condition is such that pain and effort are not just symptoms which can be removed without changing life itself; they are rather modes in which life itself, together with the necessity to which it is bound, makes itself felt. For mortals, the 'easy life of the gods' would be a lifeless life."** — Hannah Arendt

How timely: just before sitting down to write my impression of Patricia Cronin's latest undertaking—a solo Collateral Event of the 56th Venice Biennale at Chiesa di San Gallo, the smallest church in Venice—I received the good news that the Supreme Court ruled by a 5-to-4 vote the right to same-sex marriage nationwide (Friday, June 26, 2015). It's extraordinarily timely because embedded in the depth of Cronin's conscience is the singular aspiration as an artist to advocate for greater women's rights, a struggle more than a century in the making.

Her work *Memorial To A Marriage* was a symbolic declaration of equal rights, made for and displayed on a burial plot that she and her partner, the artist Deborah Kass, purchased at Woodlawn Cemetery in the Bronx in 2002. There is a pictorial continuity in her different bodies of work that welds them together in a synthesis of form and content. For example, from her past ambitious projects such as *Harriet Hosmer: Lost and Found* (2009), *Dante: The Way of All Flesh* (2012), and *Machines, Gods and Ghosts* (2013), all of which re-examine past narratives to amplify still-relevant issues of womanhood, the artist has recently turned her intense focus to

current events concerning girlhood through her *Shrine for Girls, Venice*. By activating the church's natural structure and spiritual atmosphere with minimal intervention, Patricia has been able to create a haunting installation that reveals her compassion and capacity to absorb and repurpose the pain inflicted by men's violence upon young girls around the world.

Having followed Cronin's work for quite some time, I've come to realize that two distinct components simultaneously resonate in her work: Cronin constructs representational images to document fact while, at the same time, emanating an internal light that engenders abstract, ghost-like images, whether seen, as in the case of her *Machines, Gods and Ghosts* project, or not seen, as in the case of *Memorial To A Marriage*. In the latter work, a commitment to love and death generates an invisible spirit, sensitively observed by Helen Molesworth: "[T]here it sits in a kind of obdurate grandness, awaiting its ultimate activation, its shift in temporality from anticipatory to eternal." This invisible spirit seems to come and go in accordance with the artist's visceral response to her surroundings. Mediating between figuration and abstraction, between the concrete and ethereal, between ghost and spirit, between the private and the universal, Patricia has again shifted to the latter for the sake of bringing the public attention to one of humanity's greatest tragedies: In *Shrine for Girls, Venice* the empty garments—unworn hijabs from Africa, saris from India, and aprons from the U.K.—are placed on the three respective altars in Chiesa di San Gallo. Lush heaps of fuchsia and violet rest in the slate-gray environment, while small, poignant photos placed off the center of each pile evoke three horrific atrocities: the 276 schoolgirls kidnapped by Boko Haram in Nigeria; the two teen cousins gang-raped, murdered, and hung from a tree in India; and the young women forced into labor at the Magdalene asylums and laundries in Ireland. From this presentation in Venice, their spirits rise into the invisible vapor we all breathe, reminding us that past and present crimes against women and girls are a perpetual weight on our collective conscience, and that this gesture of remembrance is part of an insistence on ending the demonic abuse and societal discrimination against girls, women, and all repressed members of humanity.

———

Patricia Cronin
Shrine for Girls, Venice:
A Work for Reflection

Ludovico Pratesi

American artist Patricia Cronin presents an environmental site specific installation in the Church of San Gallo in Venice, a strongly mystical place and for many years devoted to the display of contemporary art. The work expresses an emphasis on symbolic and synesthetic meanings where ritual, sacred offerings and votive relics come together in a sublime relationship that exalts humanity over the divine, and lauds woman, her strength and her life.

The Meaning

Shrine for Girls, Venice represents the construction of a place where memories are given life, where value is offered to the stories of women who experience daily and directly what it means, now as in the past, to be represented by a female identity which is often uncomfortable, misunderstood and even stripped of its universal significance. Patricia Cronin gives the spectator the possibility to motivate a private and personal lay ritual, moving and pausing between three stations, the three altars of the Church of San Gallo.

In *Shrine for Girls, Venice* each altar becomes a place to stop and observe, discovering among the pile of garments not only the inexorable loss of certainties and a sense of abandon often experienced by women, but also a new and efficient stimulus to react against the conditions that negate the inalienable right to be woman.

The protagonists of Patricia Cronin's work are the garments worn by women from around the world; they are infused with a renewed energy and vitality with a force that comes from the light that surrounds, permeates and unites them: three piles of clothes that exist in harmony with the space to express together the new sense of solidarity and understanding of the diverse exprinces expressed by the artist. In this way *Shrine for Girls, Venice* is returned to the public, the ceremony becomes a tribute to women, where the bodies themselves, and therefore their garments, spectacularly and elegantly represent feminine beauty with that innocence that describes perfectly the identity of a young woman.

The Works

The itinerary initiates the ritual, moving from the high altar where the gathered and illuminated saris silently and impetuously tell the stories of the adolescent Indian girls through a theatical light that emphasizes the brilliant color of the garments. The traditional sari has the capacity to express the charismatic beauty of Indian women, at the same time revealing their often daily abuses and mistreatments.

Celebrating women, the artist places on the altar of Saint Veneranda 276 veils—the Islamic hijab—as a dramatic tribute to the 276 students kidnapped in 2014 by the jihadist militants Boko Haram, in Nigeria. That tragedy persists in our memory through the vision of those same garments that covered and protected the young Nigerian women in those terrifying moments.

The altar of the Madonna del Buon Conisglio (Madonna of the Good Council), the third and last altar of the church, is dedicated to the memory of the girls who lived the dramatic experience of the Magdalene Laundries of late–19th century Ireland, where refuge was offered to prositutes. The women "sinners" were given shelter in exchange for unpayed work in the laundries, later transformed into a place of reclusion for any woman considered guilty: young mothers, rape victims, mentally ill, and orphans.

Shrine for Girls, Venice is a hymn to woman, to her often inexpressed potential. This still very current reality is worthy of artistic expression. Patricia Cronin bases her creative research on the historical and cultural female identity and the rights of women through a refined poetic language that moves from the classicism of the forms to the conceptual experimentation to the reduction of the language to powerful symbols.

The installation in the Church of San Gallo represents the construction of a ceremonial place where the expressed ritual is the consecration of an historical and current reality that relates to the beauty and power of young women.

———

left **Chibok students kidnapped by Boko Haram in Nigeria**, 2015

center **Magdalene Laundry in England**, early twentieth century

right **Cousins raped and lynched in the village of Katra, Uttar Pradesh state in India**, 2015

Patricia Cronin's Social Sculpture: Shrine for Girls

Maura Reilly

In 2014, American artist Patricia Cronin was en route to Italy when she found herself sobbing through Stephen Frears' film *Philomena*, the 2013 biopic about a woman searching for her son, whom she was forced by nuns at an Irish convent to give up for adoption. Having grown up Irish Catholic in New England, Cronin was shocked that she knew nothing about the Magdalene Laundries and was incredibly moved. The month before, she had read about the 276 teenage girls kidnapped from a secondary school by Islamist terrorist group Boko Haram in Nigeria, and, a short time later, about two young female cousins in Northern India who had been gang-raped and then lynched.

"I couldn't get the girls out of my head," Cronin says of all the brutalized females. "Every day you wake up and there's another horrible news story about violence."

Back in her Brooklyn studio she had been hard at work on a series of sculptures about the global crisis in masculinity, with references to deposition scenes (of what she calls the most famous male body in western art at his most "hopeless moment")—a series that was in part inspired by Hal Foster's review of three new Medieval and Renaissance art history books in the *London Review of Books*. But, Cronin recalls, "I thought, why am I focusing on men when I really should be focusing on the women. They really need a shrine. A shrine!" It was a eureka moment, which led to Cronin's Venice Biennale solo exhibition, *Shrine for Girls, Venice*—a "collateral" show to the national pavilions, organized by Italian curator Ludovico Pratesi. (Collateral exhibitions are chosen by the Venice Biennale Artistic Director, this year—Okwui Enwezor—as well as relate to the exhibition's overarching theme, which seeks to articulate "the current disquiet of our time.")

Located in the tiny 16th-century Church of San Gallo, Cronin's *Shrine for Girls, Venice*, transforms the deconsecrated church into a site of what she calls "global bereavement" for the world's countless abused girls. The installation itself sits on three altars, each honoring young girls who have been mistreated. As you enter the church, the altar on the left displays black-

and violet-colored hijabs, representing the mass kidnapping of the Nigerian schoolgirls by Boko Haram in 2014. Most have never been seen since. It is feared, as reported by other girls previously held captive in the area, that they have been killed, repeatedly raped, sold as sex slaves, and/or forcibly married to the terrorists. The only public "trace" of the girls to-date comes in the form of a widely disseminated photograph in which they sit on the ground in a semi-circle, clad in Islamic dress, which is featured as a tiny framed photograph on the altar beside the pile of hijabs.

The central altar displays a mass of brightly colored traditional saris worn by girls in India, two of which were gang raped and hung from a mango tree in 2014. When the girls went missing, one of their fathers immediately asked the police for help; they refused and ridiculed him because the family was of a lower caste. When the bodies were discovered the next day, angry villagers silently protested the police inaction by refusing to allow the bodies to be cut down from the tree. Some took photographs of the bodies swaying gently in a breeze as testament to the horror, one of which is placed in a tiny frame on the altar. (India's "rape problem" was thrown into high relief in 2013 when a 23-year-old physiotherapy student on a bus heading back from a movie with a male friend was gang raped and later died from her injuries—an incident that threw India into the global spotlight.)

The right altar displays a pile of monochromatic aprons and uniforms, signifying the gross mistreatment of girls at the secretive Magdalene Asylums and Laundries, forced labor institutions for young women in Ireland, the UK and America that closed only as recently as 1996, and at which they suffered physical and psychological abuse from the nuns and priests. Sentenced to a life of labor, the Catholic Church believed that through suffering and hard work for the greater glory of God, the girls might find salvation in heaven. As a reference point, Cronin has placed a small historical black and white photograph of a working laundry on the altar beside the aprons. (The photograph that accompanies each pile of clothes is critical to the installation. It allows for the specificity of the three subjects to be legible. As Cronin explains, "I lure my audience into the church by elegantly arranging the chromatically rich saris on the central altar, they move

closer out of curiosity and then notice a small framed photograph to the side and all becomes clear. With such disturbing content I thought it was important not to beat them up with it, but to let their own individual emotional/psychological arch take place.")

Together, the three altars—each dramatically spot lit from above—pack a potent political punch, inviting visitors to reflect, pray, and grieve. The installation as a whole commemorates these three groups of girls as "secular martyrs," persecuted simply because of their sex—because they were female. As Cronin explains, "Since their bodies weren't treated with dignity while they were alive, and their bodies are missing or murdered, I consider the girls as martyrs and their clothing as relics. Unlike religious martyrs, however, there is no glory in their death, no otherworldly triumph."

While there are many historical examples of secular martyrs depicted in a fine art context—one need only think of Goya's *Third of May 1808* (1814–15) or David's *Death of Marat* (1793), for instance—Cronin takes a different approach altogether. Instead of referencing Christian iconography directly—e.g. crucifixion and deposition scenes—she has instead opted for a less obvious, metaphorical representation. In other words, her secular martyrs are presented as *absent presences*. As she explains, "Their bodies are gone. The idea then of looking at clothing without bodies inside them seemed to me a poetic, powerful and poignant metaphor." In other words, Cronin has chosen not to re-present the violence perpetrated against these young women but has instead relied on the metaphorical potentiality of her medium (clothing) and site (church). Together they produce a palpable absent-presence

Jacques-Louis David (1748–1825), *Marat's Death*, 1793, oil on canvas, Collection Musees Royaux des Beaux-Arts de Belgique, Brussels, Belgium

that speaks louder than if she had chosen to represent the violence outright. However, one might ask: As an artist, how does one depict a widespread epidemic like the global violence against women? How can one represent kidnappings, rapes, lynchings, murders and other atrocities without embracing age-old stereotypes, which some may find titillating?

The history of Western art, for instance, inspired in classical antiquity by the stories of Ovid and others, and later by the numerous martyrdoms of Christian saints, and above all, by the Passion and crucifixion of Christ, has been filled with images of tortured, raped, and brutalized women. One thinks of Titian's *Rape of Europa* (1562) and Delacroix's *Abduction of Rebecca* (1846) and of the countless images of nymphs beings raped by satyrs. One thinks, too, of Veronese's heart-rending image of Saint Agatha holding a bloody cloth up to her chest after the cutting off of her breasts by the pagan executioner, but there are many, many others, like Saint Catherine broken at the Wheel or Saint Lucy having her eyes plucked out. Although meant to inspire awe

and pity—which they well may have—they also, consciously or not, must have produced a frisson of sexual pleasure in male (heterosexual) believers who got turned on by the depiction of the abuse and suffering of pretty women, as movie-goers today enjoy snuff and slasher films or other violent genres in which the brutalization of women is the featured dish on the menu.

It is this tradition of images of male domination that contemporary women artists like Cronin face up to and create alternatives for, transvaluating the outright enjoyment of women's pain and abjection that has characterized so much of the male dominated art of tradition. While many artists, writers and film directors do not

Titian (Tiziano Vecellio) (1488–1576), *Rape of Europa*, 1559–62, oil on canvas, Collection Isabella Steward Gardner Museum, Boston shy away from showing violence against women in all its goriness—as in *The Accused* (1988), Yinka Shonibare's *Gallantry and Criminal Conversation* (2002), or television's *Game of Thrones*—others are standing the tradition of male domination on its head, refusing the implications of male sexual enjoyment and aesthetic delectation implicit in both the abject victim and the classical nude of the past, and constructing new, often transgressive meanings around the feminist representation of the body, male and female. For instance, in a year long performance titled *Carry That Weight* (2014–15), artist Emma Sulkowicz chose to "carry" the mattress upon which she was raped, symbolizing the rape without depicting it outright.

The dilemma of how to represent the (ostensibly) un-representable is also one tackled by artist Ken Gonzales-Day, whose interest lies, in part, with the history of lynching in America. Unlike the horrifyingly realistic depiction of the lynching of Solomon Northup in the film *Twelve Years a Slave* (2014), for example—during which the main character chokes for breath, a rope tight around his neck, while he desperately tries to prop himself up by his toes that are sinking into a muddy ground—Gonzales-Day presents enlarged reproductions of historical postcards of lynchings in which the hanged body has been literally erased from the photograph. The absent-presence is loud and clear. By erasing the bodies, Gonzales-Day shifts the focus onto both the lynch mob spectators and onto the manner in which history and popular narratives of the West have "forgotten" these events. He points to the invisibility itself, thus bringing attention by memorializing the tragedy. In doing so, Gonzales-Day asks viewers to question cultural memory. And, as with Cronin's installation, one wonders who becomes the subject of the image in the body's absence? Does it flip the spotlight onto the audience? Yes, it does, as it should. Cronin's installation, like Gonzales-Day's series, reminds us that these are not isolated incidents of kidnapping, rape and lynching. These offences are rampant, and we all play a part in their continuation by not intervening in the injustices.

Indeed the numbers involved in abuses against women around the world are staggering. As Cronin asks, "What do you do with the statement 110,000,000 women are missing? That's what Amartya Sen, economist and winner of the Nobel Prize, said in 1990.[1] What do you do with that number?" Every day millions of women and girls worldwide experience violence. The statistics reported by the World Health Organization (WHO), United Nations Committee on Women, and Amnesty International demonstrate convincingly that violence against women is *a global epidemic*. In 2014, for instance, the WHO estimated that one in three women around the world is subject to sexual violence at some point in her life. Every year, about 14 million girls under the age of 18 are given away as child brides, and an additional 4 million women and girls are bought and sold into slavery. And according to the United Nations, at least 125 million girls in Africa and the Middle East have undergone female genital mutilation (FGM).[2]

Equally troubling is the fact that some of these abusive acts have been justified using religious doctrine. (For instance, FGM is excused by some Muslim communities under the banner of religion, especially in Africa.) Even Former US President Jimmy Carter has argued that male religious leaders have been falsely interpreting holy teachings for centuries in order to subjugate women on the grounds of religion or tradition, as if prescribed by a Higher Authority. He furthers, "Their continuing choice [to discriminate] provides the foundation or justification for much of the pervasive persecution and abuse of women throughout the world. This is in clear violation not just of the Universal Declaration of Human Rights but also the teachings of Jesus Christ, the Apostle Paul, Moses and the prophets, Muhammad, and founders of other great religions—all of whom have called for proper and equitable treatment of *all* the children of God."[3] In other words, according to Carter, prejudice based on one's sex is irrational and immoral.

Unfortunately, society has become desensitized to the rampant abuse and violence against women. As Cronin explains, "We tend to accept the idea of violence against women as 'just the way things are'—part of the status quo. Our 24 hour new cycle times delivers such tragedy and devastation all the time that it becomes easy to numb yourself to the reality of relentless human cruelty. My goal here is to 'un-numb' people, to get them to see what is really happening to women and girls all around the world."

Shrine for Girls, Venice, then, is a fiercely political work, produced by an artist who has not shied from controversial subjects in the past. In the mid-1990s Cronin exhibited a series of pornographic watercolors depicting lesbian sex, which functioned to reclaim lesbian subjectivity

from the traditionally (heterosexual) male producer/consumer of such imagery. In 2000, she produced a series of paintings of what she calls "yuppy porn"—pictures of luxury homes found in Sotheby's real estate catalogues—which are about materialism and desire.[4] Then, in 2002, the artist unveiled her masterpiece, *Memorial to a Marriage*, a monumental marble sculpture of Cronin with her life-partner (now wife), artist Deborah Kass, who are depicted lying in a tender embrace, their nude bodies partially draped with a sheet, their eyes closed in eternal slumber. The monumental work (a bronze version) is installed on their burial plot at the Woodlawn Cemetery in the Bronx. Produced before gay marriage was legal any where in the United States and nine years before the couple married—on July 24, 2011, the first day it was legal to do so in New York—it serves as "an emphatically romantic protest."[5] The sculpture is based on an infamous erotic painting created by 19th-century French painter, Gustave Courbet, titled *The Sleepers* (1866).[6] (The painting was commissioned by the Turkish

top: Patricia Cronin (1963–), *Memorial To A Marriage*, 2002, marble

bottom: Gustave Courbet (1819–1877), *The Sleepers*, 1866, oil on canvas, Collection Petit Palais, Paris

ambassador, Khalil Bey, who also owned Courbet's pornographic painting, *Origin of the World* [1866].) When the painting went up for sale in the 1880s, it caused a public scandal, and furthered Courbet's reputation as a radical. Cronin's usurpation of this now well known painting, made *for* a man and *by* a man, signifies her own radicality. Her appropriation situates her squarely in relation to a famous 19th-century canonical artist, as she inserts herself into a canon that has historically excluded lesbians, in particular, and women, in general. From a feminist perspective, it also functions to re-frame meaning in her own terms, as an "authentic" versus fictional lesbian depiction. By re-presenting herself and her lover as Courbet's couple, Cronin recovers lesbian subject matter from art history, and re-inscribes lesbian subjectivity into a painting (that had lacked it originally).

Cronin's next major project was equally political. While researching mortuary sculptures for *Memorial to a Marriage*, Cronin had encountered the work of a 19th-century American woman artist named Harriet Hosmer, whom she had never heard of before. Intrigued, she spent a year in Italy, from 2006–7, on the prestigious Rome Prize at the American Academy in Rome, meticulously studying Hosmer, who, like many male American artists of her time, went abroad to perfect her craft. When Hosmer began winning major sculpture commissions, encroaching on their turf, her male rivals waged an outright smear campaign. (Indeed, so shockingly negative were the barbs hurled at Hosmer during her lifetime that Cronin felt compelled to document the statements in a book, *The Zenobia Scandal: A Meditation on Male Jealousy*, which she published in 2013.) For her Hosmer project, Cronin published a catalogue raisonné,

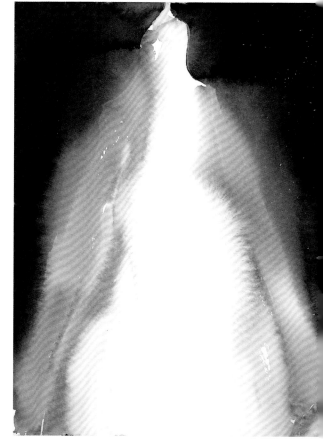

Patricia Cronin (1963–), *Queen of Naples Ghost*, 2007, watercolor on paper

for which she researched and wrote the catalogue entries, as well as produced a black-and-white watercolor of each Hosmer work she could identify, and spectral images for the ones she could not track down. It now functions as the definitive scholarly text on Hosmer. As a counter-hegemonic project, then, *Harriet Hosmer: Lost and Found, A Catalogue Raisonné*, calls special attention to work by women as cultural producers—Cronin's as well as that of Harriet Hosmer.

Cronin's *oeuvre* to-date has continually blurred the line between art and activism. Like her contemporaries Theaster Gates and Tania Bruguera, she is a proponent of "social practice art," which asserts that social change can indeed result from art. In the case of *Shrine for Girls, Venice*, for instance, Cronin provides her viewers with easy next steps, ways to get involved with the issues for which she advocates. Inside the church, beneath the curator's statement, Cronin lists three organizations striving to change girls' futures for the better: one is the Campaign for Female Education, which funds women's education and helps girls become leaders in sub-Saharan Africa; another, Gulabi Gang, Cronin describes as a "group of pink, sari-wearing female activists in India"; and then Justice for Magdalenes, an Ireland-based organization that works to ensure survivors of the Magdalene Laundries are acknowledged, protected and never forgotten.[7] Moreover, Cronin plans to donate 10 percent of any profits from the project to the listed associations.

Also accompanying the installation, a banner reads "Shrine for Girls" in the 14 most commonly spoken languages around the world. As Cronin puts it: "I want people to come to this venue from all over the world, and say, 'Wow, this is speaking to me, too.' But it also says, 'The problem is everywhere.'" "We all have bodies," she continues. "We're all made up of the same ingredients, bone, blood, organs, muscles, brains, and hearts, etc. The American Billionaire Warren Buffet has coined the phrase, 'ovarian lottery'. It is just a stroke of luck that I am not one of the Chibok students, Magdalene Laundry girls or one of the raped and lynched cousins in India. And just because I'm not one of them doesn't mean I shouldn't think about them, care about them, have an emotional response, or do nothing and remain silent."

After the *Shrine for Girls, Venice*'s opening in Venice, back in her Brooklyn studio, Cronin is surrounded by additional ancillary materials that relate to the project—e.g. mass media images of the Chibok girls, school pictures of the murdered Indian girls, and stunningly heroic oil and watercolor portraits of the Nigerian and Indian girls in vivid colors, as well as ghostlike ones of the women from the Magdalene laundries. She says she felt compelled to paint the portraits of *specific* individuals, as companion pieces to the piles of anonymous empty clothes. Moreover, as Cronin explains, "Spending the day painting the portraits of these dead or kidnapped girls is really difficult, but very necessary. There is something caring about quietly applying oil paint with a soft brush, pouring bowls of watercolor on smooth hot press paper." A master watercolorist, some of the portraits seem slightly out of focus, as if the subject might come closer and into focus yet never does. They are forever out of reach, it seems. Cronin's oil portraits are equally potent. In one, for instance, a portrait of one of the Chibok girls, Cronin has placed the young girl in a purple hijab against a garish, neon-yellow background. The chromatic intensity and juxtaposition of colors almost hurts the retina, as is Cronin's intention: "It should hurt to look at these images because the topic is so painful."

As a series, the watercolor and oil portraits are haunting representations of the missing, forgotten, and murdered. "Why shouldn't someone from the lowest caste in India have a beautiful portrait made?" Cronin asks. In art historical tradition, it is generally the aristocracy and the wealthy that are featured in heroic portraits, or those persons known to the artist—e.g. Cassatt's *Portrait of her Mother Reading Le Figaro* (1878) or Van Gogh's *Portrait of Postman Roulin* (1888). Very rarely, if ever, does one encounter a painted portrait of a child or teenager who has been brutalized during her short lifetime.

Mary Cassatt (1844–1926), *Mother Reading Le Figaro*, 1878, Collection Mrs. Eric de Spoelberch, Haverford, PA

When asked about her next project, Cronin replies, "My wish is to do a *Shrine for Girls* in many cities around the world, in different communities, with different clothes, producing different portraits, addressing different issues, and involving different non-profits organizations to donate some of the profits." But she will also be returning to the work she'd put on the back burner while working on *Shrine for Girls, Venice*, which will examine the current crisis in masculinity. When pressed why she felt compelled to return to it, Cronin explains, "Because it is too urgent, too necessary, and unfortunately I don't see that changing anytime soon. Every institution is failing us, all run by men: nations, governments, corporations, economic markets and policies, religions, and education and health care systems. All are dysfunctional and imploding."

The consummate political artist, I've no doubt Cronin's approach to the topic will be brilliant, sharp and intelligent. I'm already looking forward to it.

1   See: http://www.nybooks.com/articles/archives/1990/dec/20/more-than-100-million-women-are-missing/.

2   United Nations Women Committee http://www.unwomen.org/en/what-we-do/ending-violence-against-women/facts-and-figures; WHO (World Health Organization) http://www.who.int/mediacentre/factsheets/fs239/en/; http://www.thelancet.com/series/violence-against-women-and-girls.

3   Jimmy Carter, "Losing my religion for equality," *The Age*, July 15, 2009.

4   David Frankel, "Liebestod," *Patricia Cronin: Memorial To A Marriage*, Kansas City, MO: Grand Arts, 2002.

5   Julie Belcove, "Patricia Cronin and the Body Politic," *Financial Times*, May 1, 2015.

6   Incidentally, the same painting was a featured element in Deborah Kass' painting How Do I Look? (1991).

7   See: https://camfed.org/; http://www.gulabigang.in/; and http://www.magdalenelaundries.com/.

Chibok Student, 2015, oil on linen, 20 x 16 inches

below **Chibok Students**, 2015, watercolor on paper, 22 x 30 inches
facing **Chibok Students**, 2015, watercolor on paper, 30 x 22 inches

below **Murti**, 2015, watercolor on paper, 30 x 22 inches
facing **Pushpa**, 2015, watercolor on paper, 30 x 22 inches

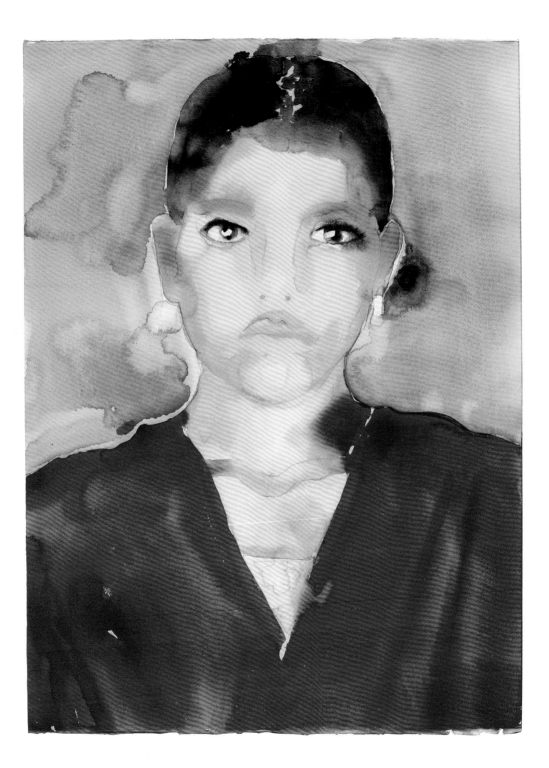

below **Magdalene Laundry Girl**, 2015, watercolor on paper, 30 x 22 inches
facing **Magdalene Laundry Girl**, 2015, watercolor on paper, 30 x 22 inches

Patricia Cronin, born in Beverly, Massachusetts, 1963

Education
_____

Brooklyn College of The City University of New York, Master of Fine Arts, Painting and Printmaking, 1988

Rhode Island College, Bachelor of Fine Arts, *cum laude*, Painting and Drawing, 1986

Skowhegan School of Painting and Sculpture, 1991

Yale University, Norfolk Summer School of Art and Music, 1985

Selected Solo Exhibitions
_____

2015
Shrine For Girls, Venice, Chiesa di San Gallo, Solo Collateral Event of the 56th International Art Exhibition – la Biennale di Venezia, Venice, Italy (catalogue)

2013
Le Macchine, Gli Dei e I Fantasmi (Machines, Gods and Ghosts), Musei Capitolini, Centrale Montemartini Museo, Rome, Italy (catalogue)

2012
Dante: The Way of All Flesh, fordPROJECT, New York, NY

Patricia Cronin: All Is Not Lost, 2000–2009, Newcomb Art Gallery, Tulane University, New Orleans, LA (catalogue)

Patricia Cronin: Bodies and Soul, Conner Contemporary Art, Washington, DC

2009–10
Patricia Cronin: Harriet Hosmer, Lost and Found, Elizabeth A. Sackler Center for Feminist Art, Brooklyn Museum, Brooklyn, NY (catalogue)

2007
An American in Rome, American Academy in Rome Art Gallery, Rome, Italy

2004
Patricia Cronin, The Domain of Perfect Affection, 1993 to 2003, UB Art Gallery, University at Buffalo, Buffalo, NY (catalogue)

2002
Memorial To A Marriage, Deitch Projects, New York, NY

Memorial To A Marriage, Grand Arts, Kansas City, MO (catalogue)

1999
The Domain of Perfect Affection, University of North Carolina, Chapel Hill, NC

1998
Tack Room, White Columns, New York, NY

Pony Tales, Arthur Roger Gallery, New Orleans, LA

1997
Pony Tales, Brent Sikkema, New York, NY

Selected Group Exhibitions
_____

2014
Global Positioning Systems: Forms of Commemoration, Pérez Art Museum Miami, Miami, FL

The Classical Nude and the Making of Queer History, Leslie-Lohman Museum of Gay and Lesbian Art, New York, NY (catalogue)

Sylvan Cemetery: Architecture, Art, and Landscape at Woodlawn, Miriam and Ira D. Wallach Art Gallery, Columbia University, New York, NY

It Begins On Paper, Catinca Tabacaru Gallery, New York, NY

Look At Me: Portraiture From Manet to the Present, Leila Heller Gallery, New York, NY

The Last Brucenniel, Vito Schnabel and The Bruce High Quality Foundation, New York, NY

Selections from the Sara M. & Michelle Vance Waddell Collection, Art Academy of Cincinnati, Cincinnati, OH

2013
Come Together: Surviving Sandy, Year 1, Dedalus Foundation, Industry City, Brooklyn, NY

NYC 1993: Experimental, Jet Set, Trash and No Star, New Museum, New York, NY

Gatsby Revisited in the Age of "The One Percent," Contemporary Art Galleries, University of Connecticut, Storrs, CT

2012
Watch Your Step, The FLAG Art Foundation, New York, NY

Twisted Sisters, Dodge Gallery, New York, NY

Permanent Collection, Kelvingrove Art Gallery and Museum, Glasgow, Scotland

2011
Sentimental Education, Gavlak Gallery, Palm Beach, FL

Annual Summer Exhibition, The Fields Sculpture Park, Omi International Arts Center, Ghent, NY

Sex Drive, Cantor Fitzgerald Gallery, Haverford College, Philadelphia, PA (traveled to Atlanta Center for Contemporary Art, Atlanta, GA)

Put Up or Shut Up, Wilkinson Gallery, New York Academy of Art, New York, NY

2010
The Narcissism of Minor Difference, The Decker Gallery, Maryland Institute College of Art, Baltimore, MD

Because We Are, Station Museum of Contemporary Art, Houston, TX

Behind the Green Door, Harris Lieberman Gallery, New York, NY

Look Again, Marlborough Gallery, New York, NY

2009
Naked, Paul Kasmin Gallery, New York, NY

Sh(OUT): Contemporary Art and Human Rights, Gallery of Modern Art (GoMA), Glasgow, Scotland

2008
Great Women Artists: Selections from the Permanent Collection, Neuberger Museum of Art, Purchase College/SUNY, Purchase, NY

Just Different, Cobra Museum, Amstelveen, The Netherlands

If Love Could Have Saved You, You Would Have Lived Forever, Bellwether, New York, NY

30th Anniversary Show, Arthur Roger Gallery, New Orleans, LA

2007
Open House: Cincinnati Collects, Contemporary Art Center, Cincinnati, OH

Trying to Land 2, Museo d'Arte Contemporanea di Roma (MACRO), Rome, Italy

Biography
_____

NeoIntegrity, Derek Eller Gallery, New York, NY

Stars and Stripes, Galleria Biagiotti Progetto Arte, Florence, Italy

2006

Twice Drawn, The Frances Young Tang Teaching Museum and Art Gallery, Skidmore College, Saratoga Springs, NY

Couples Discourse, Palmer Museum of Art, Penn State University, University Park, PA

The Title of This Show Is Not GAY ART NOW, Paul Kasmin Gallery, New York, NY

2005

High Drama: Eugene Berman and the Legacy of the Melancholic Sublime, McNay Art Museum, San Antonio, TX (traveled to Georgia Museum of Art, Athens, GA, Long Beach Museum of Art, Long Beach, CA, and Allentown Museum, Allentown, PA)

Welcome Home, Arthur Roger Gallery, New Orleans, LA

Very Early Pictures, Luckman Gallery, California State University, Los Angeles, CA (traveled to Arcadia University Art Gallery, Glenside, PA)

2004

Open House: Working in Brooklyn, Brooklyn Museum, Brooklyn, NY

2003

Collaborations with Vincent Katz, Alessandra Bonomo Gallery, Rome, Italy

Patricia Cronin & Kurt Kauper, The Armory Show, Deitch Projects, New York, NY

Arthur Roger Gallery 25th Anniversary Exhibition, Arthur Roger Gallery, New Orleans, LA

2002

Family, Aldrich Contemporary Art Museum, Ridgefield, CT

Looking at America, Yale University Art Gallery, New Haven, CT

Queer Visualities, University Art Gallery, Stony Brook University/SUNY, Stony Brook, NY

2001

Faculty Exhibition, LeRoy Neiman Gallery, School of the Arts, Columbia University, New York, NY

2000

Here Kitty, Kitty, Atlanta Contemporary Art Center, Atlanta, GA

The Standard Model: (GAME FACE), Geoffrey Young Gallery, Great Barrington, MA

1999

horsePLAY, Real Art Ways, Hartford, CT

1998

Patricia Cronin & Deborah Kass, Art Resources Transfer, Inc., New York, NY

Work on Paper, Weatherspoon Art Museum, University of North Carolina, Greensboro, NC

Drawings, GRAHAM Gallery, New York, NY

1997

The Name of the Place, Casey Kaplan Gallery, New York, NY

1996

The Strange Power of Cheap Sentiment (or a Bientot to Irony), White Columns, New York, NY

Gender, Fucked, Center on Contemporary Art, Seattle, WA

Patricia Cronin & Lee Gordon, Arthur Roger Gallery, New Orleans, LA

1995

Patricia Cronin & Lee Gordon, Richard Anderson Gallery, New York, NY

Pervert, Irvine Art Gallery, University of California, Irvine, CA

Love in the Time of Post-Feminism, Art Center/South Florida, Miami, FL

Way Cool, Exit Art/First World, New York, NY

1994

Up the Establishment: Reconstructing the Counterculture, Sonnabend Gallery, New York, NY

Stonewall 25: Imaginings of the Gay Past, Celebrating the Gay Present, White Columns, New York, NY

The Long Weekend (Ellen Cantor, Patricia Cronin, Marilyn Minter), Trial Balloon, New York, NY

Sworn Statements, Geoffrey Young Gallery, Great Barrington, MA

1993

COMING TO POWER: 25 Years of Sexually X-Plicit Art By Women, David Zwirner, New York, NY (traveled to Real Art Ways, Hartford, CT)

Love In A Cold Climate (21st Century Sex), Dooley LaCappellaine, New York, NY

The Return of the Cadavre Exquis, The Drawing Center, New York, NY

Songs of Retribution, Richard Anderson Gallery, New York, NY

Selected Awards and Fellowships

Leonard and Claire Tow Professorship, Brooklyn College, CUNY, 2013–14

Visiting Artist, American Academy in Rome, 2010, 2012, 2013, 2014

Anonymous Was A Woman Award, 2009

Brooklyn College, CUNY, Excellence in Creative Achievement Faculty Award, 2009

Civitella Ranieri Foundation Fellowship, 2009

McMillan/Stewart Award in Painting, Maryland Institute College of Art, 2008

Louis Comfort Tiffany Foundation Grant, 2007

Artist Fellowship and Deutsche Bank Fellow, New York Foundation for the Arts, 2007

Rome Prize in Visual Art, American Academy in Rome, 2006–2007

PSC-CUNY Research Award, The Research Foundation of CUNY, 2006, 2009, 2010

Distinguished Alumni Award, Rhode Island College, 2004

Artist Award, Grand Arts Foundation, 2001

Art Matters, Inc. Grant, 1996

Pollock-Krasner Foundation, Inc. Grant, 1995, 1998

Millay Colony for the Arts, Fellowship, 1988

Artists Space, Artist Grant, 1988, 1991

Collections

Deutsche Bank, New York, NY

Gallery of Modern Art, Glasgow, Scotland

Kelvingrove Art Gallery and Museum, Glasgow, Scotland

National Gallery of Art, Corcoran Collection, Washington, DC

Pérez Art Museum Miami, Miami, FL

Selected Books and Catalogues

Bui, Phong and Flam, Jack. *Come Together: Surviving Sandy*, New York: Skira Rizzoli, 2014.

Casid, Jill H., "Alter-Ovid—Contemporary Art on the Hyphen." In Miller, John F. and Carole E. Newlands, eds. *A Handbook to the Reception of Ovid*, Hoboken: John Wiley & Sons Inc., 2014.

Cronin, Patricia. *Harriet Hosmer: Lost and Found, A Catalogue Raisonné.* Milano: Charta Art Books, 2009.

———. *The Zenobia Scandal: A Meditation on Male Jealousy.* New York: ZingMagazine Books, 2013.

Deitch, Jeffrey. *Live The Art: Fifteen Years of Deitch Projects,* New York: Rizzoli, 2014.

DeWoody, Beth and Morris, Paul. "Look At Me: Portraiture From Manet to the Present." In Look At Me, Leila Heller Gallery. New York: Leila Heller Gallery, 2014.

Duncan, Michael. *High Drama: Eugene Berman and the Legacy of the Melancholic Sublime.* Manchester, VT: Hudson Hills Press, 2005.

Ebony, David, Jane Harris, Frances Richard, Meghan Dailey, and Sarah Valdez. *CURVE: The Female Nude Now.* New York: Universe, 2003.

Enwezor, Okwui. *All the World's Futures: 56 International Art Exhibition. La Biennale di Venezia,* Milano: Marsilio, 2015.

Firmin, Sandra. "Patricia Cronin's XX Portfolio." In *Patricia Cronin: The Domain of Perfect Affection: 1993 to 2003.* Buffalo, NY: UB Art Gallery, University at Buffalo, State University of New York, 2004.

Frankel, David. "Liebestod." In *Patricia Cronin: Memorial To A Marriage.* Kansas City, MO: Grand Arts, 2002.

Franklin, Carmela and Dana Prescott. *American Academy in Rome: The School of Fine Arts 2007.* Rome: Palombi Editori, 2007.

Gioni, Massimiliano; Carrion-Murayari, Gary; Moore, Jenny; and Norton, Margot, *NYC 1993: Experimental, Jet Set, Trash and No Star,* New York: New Museum, 2013.

Gross, Jennifer. *Looking At America.* New Haven, CT: Yale University Art Gallery, 2002.

Hammond, Harmony. *Lesbian Art in America.* New York: Rizzoli, 2000.

Hammond, Harmony and Catherine Lord. *Gender, Fucked.* Seattle: Center on Contemporary Art, with Bay Press, 1996.

Harithas, James and Tim Gonzalez. *Because We Are.* Houston, TX: Station Museum of Contemporary Art, 2010.

Klein, Richard, Jessica Hough, and Harry Philbrick. *Family.* Ridgefield, CT: Aldrich Museum of Contemporary Art, 2002.

Kotik, Charlotta and Tumelo Mosaka. *Open House: Working in Brooklyn,* New York: Brooklyn Museum, 2004.

Lancaster, Lex Morgan. "Close Proximity, Intimate Distance: the Abstracting Effects of Photographic Contact." In *The Wet Archive,* Chasen Museum, Madison, WI: University of Wisconsin, 2015. https://wetarchive.wordpress.com/Essays-2/.

Latimer, Tirza. "Having it Both Ways: Queer/Feminist Art/History." In Jones, Amelia and Erin Silver eds. *Sexual Differences and Otherwise: Imagining Queer Feminist Art Histories,* Manchester: Manchester University Press, 2015.

Lord, Catherine. *Pervert.* Irvine, CA: Irvine Art Gallery, University of California, 1995.

Lord, Catherine and Meyer, Richard, *Art and Queer Culture,* London: Phaidon Press, 2013.

McGlashan, Sean. *Sh(OUT): Contemporary Art and Human Rights.* Glasgow, Scotland: Modern Gallery of Art, 2009.

Miller, Peter Benson. "Roma Sparita." In *Patricia Cronin: Le Macchine, Gli Dei e I Fantasmi*, Musei Capitolini, Centrale Montimartini Museo. Milano: Silvana Editoriale, 2013.

Molesworth, Helen, "All is not lost: Love and Death in the work of Patricia Cronin." In *Patricia Cronin: All Is Not Lost*, New Orleans, LA: Tulane University, 2012.

Nemerov, Alexander, "Ghosts and Sculpture: Harriet Hosmer and Patricia Cronin." In *Patricia Cronin: All Is Not Lost*, New Orleans: Tulane University, 2012.

Pratesi, Ludovico. "Le Macchine, gli Dei e I Fantasmi: Reasons for the Exhibition." In *Patricia Cronin: Le Macchine, Gli Dei e I Fantasmi,* Musei Capitolini, Centrale Montimartini Museo. Milano: Silvana Editoriale, 2013.

Reed, Christopher. *Art and Homosexuality: A History of Ideas.* New York: Oxford University Press, 2011.

Reilly, Maura. "Preface." *Harriet Hosmer: Lost and Found, A Catalogue Raisonné.* Milano: Charta Art Books, 2009.

Robinson, Joyce Henri. *Couples Discourse.* University Park, PA: Palmer Museum of Art, with Pennsylvania State University Press, 2006.

Rosenblum, Robert. "On Patricia Cronin: From Here to Eternity." In *Patricia Cronin: The Domain of Perfect Affection: 1993 to 2003.* Buffalo, NY: UB Art Gallery, University at Buffalo, State University of New York, 2004.

Sandell, Richard. "Museums and the Human Rights Frame." In *Museums, Equality and Social Justice,* edited by Eithne Nightingale and Richard Sandell. London: Routledge, 2012.

Smyth, Cherry. *Damn Fine Art: New Art by Lesbians.* London: Cassell Publishers, 1996.

Berry, Ian and Jack Shear. *Twice Drawn: Modern and Contemporary Drawings in Context.* Saratoga Springs, NY: The Frances Young Tang Teaching Museum and Art Gallery, Skidmore College, with DelMonico Prestel Press, 2011.

Villa, Rocío de la. "Artistas Heroínas." In *Heroínas.* Madrid: Museo Thyssen-Bornemisza, 2011.

Wagner, Frank. *Just Different.* Amstelveen: Cobra Museum, 2008.

Interviews

Bui, Phong. "Patricia Cronin in Conversation with Phong Bui," The *Brooklyn Rail*, November 2012.

Castro, Jan Garden. "Making The Personal Monumental: A Conversation With Patricia Cronin." *Sculpture*, January/February 2003.

Cronin, Patricia. "A Conversation on Lesbian Subjectivity and Painting with Deborah Kass." In *M/E/A/N/I/N/G: An Anthology of Artists' Writings, Theory, and Criticism,* edited by Susan Bee and Mira Schor. Durham, NC: Duke University Press, 2003.

Dalamangas, Rachel Cole. Interview: Patricia Cronin. Zing Chat, April 2013. http://www.zingmagazine.com/chat.html.

Gonzalez Pendergast, Isabel. "Patricia Cronin's 'Shrine For Girls,' Venice Biennale," *LITRO Magazine*, June 8, 2015. http://www.litro.co.uk/2015/06/patricia-cronins-shrine-for-girls-venice-biennale/.

Haynes, Clarity. "From Grief to Action: Patricia Cronin on Her 'Shrine for Girls,'" *Hyperallergic*, May 25, 2015. http://hyperallergic.com/208620/from-grief-to-action-patricia-cronin-on-her-shrine-for-girls/.

Kass, Deborah. "Conversation: Patricia Cronin and Deborah Kass." New York: *Art Resources Transfer, Inc.*, 1998.

Langer, Cassandra. "The Second Life of Harriet Hosmer: Cassandra

Bibliography

Langer Talks with an Artist's Artist." *Gay & Lesbian Review Worldwide* 17, no. 1, 2010.

Mayes, Tom. "Art in Old Places: Artist Patricia Cronin Confronts the Present with the Past." *National Trust for Historic Preservation Blog*, February 7, 2014. http://blog.preservationnation.org/2014/02/07/art-old-places-artist-patricia-cronin-confronts-present-past/#.UzM-WutKL9I.

McNay, Anna and Kennedy Martin. "Patricia Cronin: 'A Silent Protest Can Be Quite Powerful,'" *Studio International*, June 23, 2015. http://www.studiointernational.com/index.php/patricia-cronin-shrine-for-girls-venice-biennale-video-interview.

Nikulina, Svetlana. "Croninatrix: An Interview with New York Artist Patricia Cronin," *Book Magazine* (Russia), Porno Issue, Issue #5, Jan-Feb, 2014. http://bookmagazinerussia.ru/porno/interview/croninatrix

Selected Articles and Reviews

Andioni, Guila. "Patricia Cronin: Presenze e assenze." *Artibune.com*, November 8, 2013.

Asper, Colleen. "Found in Translation – Chasing Dante's Inferno with Mary Jo Bang and Patricia Cronin." *TheWeeklings.com*, March 31, 2012. http://casper/2013/03/31/found-in-translation/.

———. "If Love Could Have Saved You, You Would Have Lived Forever." *Artcritical*, August 13, 2008. http://www.artcritical.com/2008/09/14/if-love-could-have-saved-you-you-would-have-lived-forever-curated-by-becky-smith/.

Atkins, Robert. "Goodbye Lesbian/Gay History, Hello Queer Sensibility: Mediating on Curatorial Practice." *Art Journal* 55, no. 4. Winter 1996.

———. "Very Queer Indeed." *Village Voice*, January 31, 1995.

Azzarello, Nina. "Patricia Cronin Remembers the Repressed with Shrine For Girls." *Design Boom*, May 4, 2015. http://www.designboom.com/art/patricia-cronin-venice-shrine-for-girls-venice-art-biennale-04-05-2015/.

Best, Kenneth. "Contemporary Art Galleries Revisit Gatsby with 'Age of the One Percent' Exhibit." *UConn Today*, April 1, 2013. http://today.uconn.edu/blog/2013/04/contemporary-art-galleries-revisit-gatsby-with-age-of-the-one-percent-exhibit/.

Belcove, Julie. "Patricia Cronin and the Body Politic: the American Artist on the Essential Role of Art in Feminism." *Financial Times*, May 2, 2015.

Blizzard, Christina. "Glasgow's New Auld Vibe: Industrial Port City Now Bustling Cultural Hub." *Toronto Sun*, June 14, 2015. http://www.torontosun.com/2015/06/11/glasgows-new-auld-vibe-industrial-port-city-now-bustling-cultural-hub.

Bolcer, Julie. "Love and Marriage, On Display For Eternity." *Advocate*, September 21, 2011.

Britt, Douglas. "Exhibit on 'Queer Identity' Requires Unusual Preparations." *Houston Chronicle*, June 18, 2010.

———. "Gay Identity Unfiltered." *Houston Chronicle*, June 18, 2010.

———. "Houston Was Treated To Great Art Shows in 2010." *Houston Chronicle*, December 21, 2010.

Brookhardt, Eric D. "Review: work by Patricia Cronin at Newcomb Gallery." *Best of New Orleans*, May 31, 2012. http://www.bestofneworleans.com/blogofneworleans/Archive/2012/05/31review-work-by-patricia-cronin-at-newcomb-gallery.

Budick, Ariella. "NYC 1993: Experimental Jet Set, Trash and No Star, New Museum, New York." *Financial Times*, February 27, 2013.

Buglioni, Maila. "Patricia Cronin alla Centrale Montemartini: Incorporee Figure." *Art A Part of Cult(ure)*, November 20, 2013.

"Bush a Roma: Patricia Cronin, L'Arte Della Sensualita." *Pittura Oggi*, June 9, 2007.

Canning, Susan. "Tack Room." *Sculpture*, October 1998.

Casadio, Giovanna. "Per La First Lady arte e niente shopping." *La Repubblica*, June 9, 2007.

Castle, Terry. "The Woman in the Gallery." *The New York Review of Books*, August 14, Volume LXI, Number 13, 2014.

Castro, Jan Garden. "Open House: Working in Brooklyn." *Sculpture*, January/February 2005.

Caswell-Pearce, Sara. "The Fine Art of Collecting [De Mystified]." *EXPRESS Cincinnati*, February 2014.

Cembalest, Robin. "Venice Highlights 2015: Pavilions and Collateral Events." *Art in America*, May 11, 2015.

Cirinei, Cecilia. "In Mostra Patricia Cronin Con Sei Opera Monumentali." *la Repubblica*, October 14, 2013.

Cole, Michal. "Venice Biennale Satellite Exhibitions: Following The Political Trail." *Artlyst*, May 7, 2015. http://www.artlyst.com/articles/venice-biennale-satellite-exhibitions-following-the-political-trail.

Compton, Kelly. "Contemporary Masterworks on View Nationwide." *Fine Art Connoisseur*, Vol. 9, no.3, June 2012.

Cotter, Holland. "Brooklyn-ness, a State of Mind and Artistic Identity in the Un-Chelsea." *The New York Times*, April 16, 2004.

———. "Gay Pride (and Anguish) Around the Galleries." *The New York Times*, June 24, 1994.

———. "The Name of the Place." *The New York Times*, January 31, 1997.

———. "Patricia Cronin and Deborah Kass." *The New York Times*, April 17, 1998.

———. "Patricia Cronin and Lee Gordon." *The New York Times*, May 5, 1995.

———. "Patricia Cronin: 'Harriet Hosmer, Lost and Found.'" *The New York Times*, June 18, 2009.

———. "Tammy Rae Carland." *The New York Times*, December 5, 2002.

———. "A Tour Through Chelsea, The New Center of Gravity." *The New York Times*, May 15, 1998.

———. "Trade." *The New York Times*, February 25, 2005.

———. "What "F" Word?." *The New York Times*, March 7, 2007.

Criara, Silvia. "Gli Artivisti." *Marie Claire Italia*, May 2015.

Cronin, Patricia. "Dante's Inferno/The Way of All Flesh." *M/E/A/N/I/N/G*, 2011. http://writing.upenn.edu/epc/meaning/05/meaning-online-5.html#cronin.

———. "Harriet Hosmer: Catalogue Raissonné." *BOMB*, Fall 2008.

———. "Linda Nochlin." *The Brooklyn Rail*, July/August 2015.

———. "Memorial to a Marriage." *Public Art Review* 22, no. 1, Fall/Winter 2010.

———. "Obsessions: What A Girl Wants." *CAA Art Journal* 60, no. 4, Winter 2001.

———, ed. "Representing Lesbian Subjectivities." Special issue, *Art Papers* 18, no. 6, November/December 1994.

———. "'Til Death Do Us Part." *Huffington Post*, October 4, 2011. http://www.huffingtonpost.com/patricia-cronin/post_2511_b_995251.html.

Cupailuolo, Christine. "Brave Grave." *Ms. Magazine*, Spring 2004.

Curtis, Cathy. "Exposing 'Pervert,' UCI Show Reveals Fresh Views of Homosexuality That Are No Threat to the Open-Minded." *Los Angeles Times*, May 3, 1995.

Dalamangas, Rachel Cole. "Deja Zing: Patricia Cronin Takes a View from Above in Luxury Real Estate Paintings." *Zing*: April 30, 2014. http://www.zingtumblr.com/post/84390311303/deja-zing-patricia-cronin-takes-a-view-from-above-in.

Denson, G. Roger. "When Walls Come Falling Down: Left Political Art Timeline, 1989–2000." *The Huffington Post*, April 16, 2012. http://www.huffingtonpost.com/g-roger-denson/9892000_b_1422848.html.

DePalma, Anthony. "A Daring (and Icy) Duet." *The New York Times*, February 23, 2003.

Di Forti, Massimo. "I Fantasmi di Patricia Cronin alla Centrale Montemartini." *Il Messaggero*, November 11, 2013.

Drucks, Achim. "Desperately Seeking Harriet: The American Artist Patricia Cronin on the Trail of a Forgotten Sculptress." *Deutsche Bank Art Mag* 43 (July 17–October 8, 2007). http://db-artmag.com/archiv/2007/e/3/5/542.html.

Duray, Dan. "Look at This! Patricia Cronin at fordProject." *GalleristNY.com*, November 29, 2012. http://galleristny.com/2012/11/look-at-this-patricia-cronin-at-ford-project/.

Ebony, David. "The Melancholy Gang: Eugene Berman and His Circle." *Art in America*, March 2006.

Editors. "11 Artists Who Helped Pave the Way to Marriage Equality." *ArtSy*, July 1, 2015. https://www.artsy.net/article/artsy-editorial-11-artists-who-helped-pave-the-way-to?utm_source=Current+Users&utm_campaign=77548e6f15-Weekly+email+249_Editorial39&utm_medium=email&utm_term=0_c67eb1f0a4-77548e6f15-412088921.

Editors. "Venice Biennale Guide 2015." *The Art Newspaper*, May 2015.

Ferrario, Rachel. "Il Colore Dei Versi." *Corriere Della Sera*, December 23, 2003.

Finch, Charlie. "The Lady Hosmer." *Artnet*, May 29, 2009. http://www.artnet.com/magazineus/features/finch/patricia-cronin5-29-09.asp.

———. "A Visit With Deb and Pattie." *Artnet*, January 18, 2006. http://www.artnet.com/magazineus/features/finch/finch1-18-06.asp.

Frank, Priscilla. "Heartbreaking 'Shrine For Girls' Pays Tribute To Young Female Martyrs Around The World." *The Huffington Post*, April 14, 2015. http://www.huffingtonpost.com/2015/04/14/patricia-cronin-shrine-for-girls-venice_n_7058554.html.

Frankel, David. "Pony Tales." *Artforum*, April 1997.

"Galleries - Patricia Cronin." *New Yorker*, December 2, 2002.

Gayford, Martin. "Martin Gayford Finds a Few Nice Paintings Amid the Dead Trees, Old Clothes and Agitprop of the Venice Biennale." *The Spectator*, May 16, 2015.

Gehman, Geoff. "Controversial Tombstone a Monument to the Triumph of Love." *LeHigh Valley (PA) Morning Call*, February 5, 2006.

Gleadell, Colin, "Venice Biennale: Gas Masks, Marx, and Cigarettes in the Wrong Places." *CNN*, May 13, 2015.

Gronlund, Melissa. "Art Talk: Plot Twist." *ARTnews*, January 2003.

Ha, J. "Artists in Need of Career Guidance Welcome." *The Art Newspaper*, June 18, 2014.

Halperin, Julia. "A Curator's Diary: Armory Week with FLAG Director Stephanie Roach." *Artinfo.com*, March 9, 2012.

Haveles, Kate. "Beyond the Biennale: 21 Top Shows to See Around Venice." *Artsy*, May 3, 2015. www.artsy.net/article/artsy-editorial-venice-biennale-2015-21-top-museum-shows-events.

Hess, Elizabeth. "Basic Instincts." *Village Voice*, June 1, 1993.

Hirsch, Faye. "Patricia Cronin, The Domain of Perfect Affection 1993-2003." *Art in America*, October 2004.

———. "Seeing Queerly." *Art in America*, February 4, 2011. http://www.artinamericamagazine.com/features/seeing-queerly/.

Jenkins, Mark. "Patricia Cronin." *The Washington Post*, February 24, 2012.

Johnson, Ken. "If Love Could Have Saved You, You Would Have Lived Forever." *The New York Times*, July 25, 2008.

———. "The Artist Next Door: 'Crossing Brooklyn,' Local Talent at Brooklyn Museum." *The New York Times*, October 2, 2014.

Johnson, John. "Reviewed: Patricia Cronin at Conner Contemporary." *Washington City Paper*, February 15, 2012.

Jun, Christine. "The DA-ZED Guide to Porn Art, As Cameron's Porn Ban Becomes Policy, We Count 26 Intersections of Radical Art and Grot." *Dazed & Confused Magazine*, August 2, 2013. http://www.dazeddigital.com/photography/article/16798/1/the-da-zed-guide-to-porn-art.

Kahn, Eve. M. "Designs That Outlived Their Benefactors." *The New York Times*, August 21, 2014.

Kalra, Vandana. "Coming Apart at the Seams: American Artist Patricia Cronin On Creating 'Shrine For Girls.'" *The Indian Express*, June 13, 2015.

Katz, Vincent. "Girlfriends: Up Close and Personal with Artist Patricia Cronin." *Paper*, April 1995.

———. "Pony Tales." *Art in America*, September 1997.

Kazad. "Violence Against Girls and Women Remembered at Venice." *Artcentron*, May 15, 2015. http://artcentron.com/2015/05/15/violence-against-girls/.

Kley, Elizabeth. "Patricia Cronin, fordPROJECT." *ARTnews*, March 2013.

Kort, Michelle. "Eternal Portrait of a Lesbian Marriage." *Ms. Magazine* (blog), September 19, 2011. http://msmagazine.com/blog/blog/2011/09/19/eternal-portrait-of-a-lesbian-marriage/.

Liebmann, Lisa. "The Best of 1998." *Artforum*, December 1998.

Lister, David. "Venice Biennale 2015: Why This Year Could Be More Political Than the General Election," *The Independent*, May 1, 2015.

MacAdam, Barbara A. "Till Death Do Us Art." *Art News*, September 2014.

Mack, Von Gerhard. "Die Kunstler Geben Sich Politisch." *NZZ am Sonntag*, May 10, 2015.

McManus, Bridget. "Afternoon Delight: A 'Bridesmaids' Blooper Reel, Out Artist Patricia Cronin's New Sculpture." *AfterEllen*, September 12, 2011. http://www.afterellen.com/column/afternoon-delight/2011-09-12

Meier, Allison. "Exhuming the Artistic Afterlife from One of NYC's Historic Cemeteries." *Hyperallergic*, September 15, 2014. http://hyperallergic.com/148447/exhuming-the-artistic-afterlife-from-one-of-nycs-historic-cemeteries/.

———. "From Courbet to the Bronx, The Love That Dare Not Speak Its Names Gets Marriage Memorial." *Hyperallergic*, October 10, 2011. http://hyperallergic.com/?s=cronin.

———. "From Da Bronx to Eternity." *Hyperallergic*, July 3, 2012. http://hyperallergic.com/53757/from-da-bronx-to-eternity/.

———. "The Tombs of Artists As a Last Statement From The Grave." *Hyperallergic*, August 1, 2013. http://hyperallergic.com/76916/the-tombs-of-artists-a-last-statement-from-the-grave/.

Meriam, Mary. "Subverting the "Girlie" Calendar: April." *Ms. Magazine Blog*, April 1, 2015. http://msmagazine.com/blog/2015/04/01/subverting-the-girlie-calendar-april/.

Miller, Paul. "Children Banned From Explicit Gallery Display." *Herald (Glasgow)*, April 9, 2009.

———. "Explicit Images To Go On Show In Gallery." *Herald (Glasgow)*, April 2, 2009.

Moon, Grace. "Art for the Weekend: Patricia Cronin, Daphne Fitzpatrick, Julia Kunin." *Velvet Park*, November 19, 2012. http://www.velvetparkmedia.com/blogs/art-weekend-patricia-cronin-daphne-fitzpatrick-julia-kunin.

———. "A Shrine For Girls, Installation by Patricia Cronin." *Velvet Park*, May 7, 2015. http://www.velvetparkmedia.com/blogs/shrine-girls-installation-patricia-cronin.

———. "Memorial to a Marriage." *Velvet Park*, September 6, 2010. http://velvetparkmedia.com/video/memorial-marriage.

———. "Velvetpark's Official Top 25 Significant Queer Women of 2012." *Velvet Park*, December 21, 2012. http://www.velvetparkmedia.com/blogs/velvetparks-official-top-25-significant-queer-women-2012.

Munoz-Alonzo, Lorena. "Artist Patricia Cronin Dedicates Altars to Suffering Girls at Venice Biennale." *Artnet*, April 7, 2015. https://news.artnet.com/in-brief/patricia-cronin-shrine-for-girls-venice-biennale-285715.

Nadelman, Cynthia. "The New Realism." *ARTnews*, December 2004.

Nania, Rachel. "Patricia Cronin Exhibits Bodies and Soul at Conner Contemporary Art." *ArtSee: Coloring DC*, February 7, 2012.

Napoleoni, Marta. "Patricia Cronin – Le Macchine, gli Dei e I Fantasmi." *Exibart.com*, November 8, 2013.

"Neoclassico: Le Macchine, Gli Gei, I Fantasmi." *IO Donna Il Femminile Del Corriere Della Sera*, October 12, 2013.

Ollman, Leah. "An Open-Armed Welcome." *Los Angeles Times*, June 4, 2004.

"Omaggio alla Hosmer di Patricia Cronin." *Corriere Della Sera*, October 7, 2013.

Paice, Kim. "Coming To Power." *Art+Text*, Fall 1993.

"Patricia Cronin, Shrine for Girls, La Biennale di Venezia, Venice." *Aesthetica*, May 27, 2015. http://www.aestheticamagazine.com/patricia-cronin-shrine-for-girls-la-biennale-di-venezia-venice/.

Pollack, Barbara. "ARTtalk: The Mane Event." *ARTnews*, November 1999.

———. "Love Potions: Art and the Heart." *ARTnews*, February 2013.

———. "1993." *Modern Weekly (China)*. April 2013.

Privato, Manuela. "L'Arte Moltiplica l'arte nella Biennale Segreta." *Il Mattino*, June 2, 2015.

Quick, Harriet. "IFashion APP." *Modern Weekly (China)*, May 25, 2015.

Reilly, Maura. "Personal But Highly Political Highlights From the 2015 Venice Biennale." *Hyperallergic*, June 22, 2015. http://hyperallergic.com/216252/personal-but-highly-political-highlights-from-the-2015-venice-biennale/.

Reyburn, Scott. "Venice Biennale Expands Its Scope," *The International New York Times*, May 8, 2015.

Rosenblum, Robert. "The Best of 2003." *Artforum*, December 2003.

Russell, Legacy. "Memorial To A Marriage: Artist Patricia Cronin Casts Eternity." *BOMBlog*, September 19, 2011. http://bombsite.com/issues/1000/articles/6090.

Russeth, Andrew. "Artists Patricia Cronin and Deborah Kass to Rest Forever in Bronx Cemetery." *New York Observer*, September 12, 2011.

———. "How Are New York's Art Types Riding Out Hurricane Sandy?." *GalleristNY.com*, October 29, 2012.

Russo, Paolo. "Gli Abiti-Denuncia di Patricia Cronin." *La Repubblica*, June 28, 2015.

Saltz, Jerry. "Forever Yours." *Village Voice*, October 29, 2003.

———. "A Year in the Life: Tropic of Painting." *Art in America*, October 1994.

Santis, Linda de. "Katz & Clemente Ecco L'unione Tra Poesia e Pittura." *La Repubblica*, December 27, 2003.

Sassi, Edoardo. "Dedicato a te, Harriet Hosmer: 'Fatasmi' d'arte nella personale di Patricia Cronin." *Corriere Della Sera*, October 11, 2013.

Scarpello, Lauren. "Review: 'Patricia Cronin: All Is Not Lost.'" *Pelican Bomb*, June 7, 2012. http://pelicanbomb.com/home/post/242.

Sheets, Hillary M. "Riffing on Forefathers and Mothers." *The New York Times*, October 26, 2012.

Short, Alice. "Warm Glow at Perez Art Museum Miami Goes Beyond South Florida Sun," *Los Angeles Times*, July 18, 2015. http://www.latimes.com/travel/la-tr-d-perez-art-museum-20150719-story.html.

Small, Rachel, "The Unsinkable Art World." *Interview*, October 2013.

Smith, Mark. "Mapplethorpe's Ugly Image Risks Pandering to Gay Stereotypes." *Herald (Glasgow)*, April 2, 2009.

Solomon, Deborah. "Bye, Hornet's Nest: It's Back to New York: Jeffrey Deitch Has Big Plans Now That He's Left Los Angeles." *The New York Times*, October 2, 2014.

Strong, Lester. "The Out 100." *Out*, December 2003.

Swanson, Carl. "Jeffrey Deitch Curates Jeffery Deitch: The Return of the Art World's Most Essential Zelig." *New York Magazine,* January 12, 2014. http://www.vulture.com/2014/01/jeffrey-deitch-returns-to-the-art-world.html.

Symonds, Alexandria. "Mickalene Thomas's Adventures in Italy." *The New York Times Magazine T Blog.* June 17, 2015. http://tmagazine.blogs.nytimes.com/2015/06/17/mickalene-thomas-italy-traveldiary/?hpw&rref=tmagazine&action=click&pgtype=Homepage&module=well-region&region=bottom-well&WT.nav=bottom-well&_r=0.

Ugolini, Paola. "L'Altra Venezia in Tre Sedi Fuori Dal Coro." *Exibart*, June 7, 2015. http://www.exibart.com/notizia.asp?IDNotizia=46017&IDCategoria=1.

Vartanian, Hrag. "Marriage Equality for All! #LoveWins." *Hyperallergic*, June 26, 2015. http://hyperallergic.com/218117/marriage-equality-for-all-lovewins/.

———. "Your Concise Guide to the 2015 Venice Biennale'" *Hyperallergic*, May 5, 2015.

Volk, Gregory. "Big Brash Borough." *Art in America*, September 2004.

Watson, Keri W., "Parody as Political Tool in Patricia Cronin's *Memorial to a Marriage." Mosaic: A Journal for the Interdisciplinary Study of Literature* 43, no. 2, 2010.

Weingarten, Judith. "Zenobia, Lost and Found." *Zenobia Empress of the East* (blog), July 10, 2009. http://judithweingarten.blogspot.com/2009/07/zenobia-lost-and-found.html.

Wolff, Rachel. "Art Talk: Neoclassic Revival." *ARTnews*, Summer 2009.

Wolin, Joseph R. "Anna Plesset, A Still Life." *Time Out New York*, February 14–20, 2013.

———. "Patricia Cronin, 'Harriet Hosmer, Lost and Found.'" *Time Out New York*, August 27, 2009.

Yablonsky, Linda. "She Digs A Pony." *Out*, December/January 1997.

———. "Remembering Murray." *Artforum*, August 30, 2007.

———. "Back to the Futures." *Artforum*, May 12, 2015. http://artforum.com/diary/id=52149

Zaytoun, Constance. "Nostalgic for a Future: Hannah Wilke's *Intra-Venus Tapes* and Patricia Cronin's *Memorial to a Marriage.*" Monuments and Moving Targets: Civic Engagement by Female Performance Artists in the 21st Century Panel, Association for Theatre in Higher Education Conference, 2012.

Phong Bui

Phong Bui is an artist, writer, independent curator and former curatorial advisor at MoMA PS1, 2007 to 2010. He is also the Co-Founder, Publisher/Editor-in-chief of the monthly journal the *Brooklyn Rail* and the publishing press *Rail Editions*, as well as the Host/Producer of " Off the Rail" on Art International Radio. He is a board member of the *Third Rail* of the Twin Cities, the *Miami Rail*, the Louis Comfort Tiffany Foundation, the Walentas/Walsh Sharpe Foundation, and the International Association of Art Critics United States Section (AICA USA). He is currently teaching graduate seminars in MFA Writing and Criticism and MFA Photography, Video, and Related Media at the School of Visual Arts.

Ludovico Pratesi

Ludovico Pratesi, one of Italy's most respected contemporary art curators and art critic for *La Repubblica* newspaper, has organized numerous museum and gallery exhibitions. He is currently the artistic director of Fondazione Pescheria in Pesaro, of the Fondazione Guastalla in Lugano, Switzerland, and of the Young Collectors Association in Rome. Former Vice President of Associazione Musei Arte Contemporana Italiana and former President of Association Internationale des Critiques d'Art (AICA Italy), he has curated shows at institutions such as Galleria Borghese and MACRO in Rome, Ny Carlsberg Glyptotek in Copenaghen, Proa Foundation in Buenos Aires, Columbia University in New York, and Crane Art Center in Philadelphia.

Maura Reilly

Maura Reilly is Chief Curator at the National Academy Museum and School in New York City. Prior to this position, she served as Professor and Chair of Art Theory at Griffith University in Australia, as Senior Curator at the American Federation of Arts, and as Founding Curator of the Sackler Center for Feminist Art at the Brooklyn Museum. She is the author of several books and has curated dozens of exhibitions internationally. For more information, please visit: www.maurareilly.com.

Contributors

Sponsors and Thanks

Major support for the *Shrine for Girls, Venice* exhibition is provided by our lead sponsors, The FLAG Art Foundation and The Fuhrman Family Foundation.

With the additional generous support of Agnes Gund, John and Amy Phelan, Jane and David Walentas, Arcadia Foundation, Lococo Fine Art Publisher, Stephanie Ingrassia, Chuck Close, Helen Stambler Neuberger and Jim Neuberger, Alice Zoloto-Kosmin, Marlies Verhoeven, Deborah Kass, George Rudenauer Consulting, Beverly Joel/pulp, ink., Sara M. and Michelle Vance Waddell, Lois Plehn, Francis J. Greenburger, Debi Sonzogni and A.G. Rosen, Craig Drill, Anonymous, Martha Macks-Kahn, Elaine Gray and Anne Belluche Cronin.

Special Thanks

The artist would like to extend special thanks to Ludovico Pratesi, Chiara Pirozzi, Phong Bui, Sara Christoph, Amanda and Glenn Fuhrman, Maura Reilly, Okwui Enwezor, Paolo Scibelli, Manuela Lucà Dazio, Don Gianmatteo Caputo, Luciana Pizzati, Ilina Udrea, Michael Hall, Annabelle's Aprons, India Sari Palace, and Maktaba Dar-Us-Salam, Inc.

How You Can Help

The Gulabi Gang is a group of Indian women activists responding to widespread domestic abuse and other violence against women in India. Recently they have gained international attention for taking matters into their own hands while the police and male-dominated society ignore and reinforce the plight of women in their country. www.gulabigang.in

Justice For Magdalenes seeks to promote and represent the interests of the Magdalene women, to respectfully promote equality and seek justice for the women formerly incarcerated in Ireland's Magdalene Laundries and to seek the establishment and improvements of support as well as advisory and re-integration services provided for survivors. www.magdalenelaundries.com

Camfed – Campaign for Female Education is an international non-profit organization tackling poverty and inequality by supporting girls to go to school and succeed, and empowering young women to step up as leaders of change. Camfed invests in girls and women in the poorest rural communities in sub-Saharan Africa, where girls face acute disadvantage, and where their empowerment is now transforming communities. www.camfed.org

With the belief that artists can be effective social entrepreneurs, Patricia Cronin is donating 10% of profits from *Shrine For Girls, Venice* to organizations that promote equality for women and girls.

Acknowledgments

Sanctuaire pour les filles   여자에 대한 신사   Παρεκκλήσι για τα κορίτσια   Kuil untuk anak peremp

Santuário para meninas   Храм для девочек   Shrine for Girls   女の子のための神社   Schrein für Mädchen   Santuari

k perempuan   Miếu thờ cho trẻ em gái   Santuario per le ragazze   ضريح للفتيات   Scrín do chailíní   女孩的神殿   Sv

ntuario de las niñas   מקדש עבור בנות   Храм за момичета   Sanctuaire pour les filles   여자에 대한 신사   Παρεκκλήσι

殿   Svatyně pro dívky   लड़कियों के लिए तीर्थ   Santuário para meninas   Храм для девочек   Shrine for Girls   女の子のた

ρεκκλήσι για τα κορίτσια   Kuil untuk anak perempuan   Miếu thờ cho trẻ em gái   Santuario per le ragazze   للفتيات

子のための神社   Schrein für Mädchen   Santuario de las niñas   מקדש עבור בנות   Храм за момичета   Sanctuaire pou

للفتي   Scrín do chailíní   女孩的神殿   Svatyně pro dívky   लड़कियों के लिए तीर्थ   Santuário para meninas   Храм

ctuaire pour les filles   여자에 대한 신사   Παρεκκλήσι για τα κορίτσια   Kuil untuk anak perempuan   Miếu thờ cho tr

ninas   Храм для девочек   Shrine for Girls   女の子のための神社   Schrein für Mädchen   Santuario de las niñas   בנות

u thờ cho trẻ em gái   Santuario per le ragazze   للفتيات   Scrín do chailíní   女孩的神殿   Svatyně pro dívky   ל

as   מקדש עבור בנות   Храм за момичета   Sanctuaire pour les filles   여자에 대한 신사   Παρεκκλήσι για τα κορίτσια

dívky   लड़कियों के लिए तीर्थ   Santuário para meninas   Храм для девочек   Shrine for Girls   女の子のための神社   Schrei

κορίτσια   Kuil untuk anak perempuan   Miếu thờ cho trẻ em gái   Santuario per le ragazze   للفتيات   Scrín do

Schrein für Mädchen   Santuario de las niñas   מקדש עבור בנות   Храм за момичета   Sanctuaire pour les filles   여ㅈ

n do chailíní   女孩的神殿   Svatyně pro dívky   लड़कियों के लिए तीर्थ   Santuário para meninas   Храм для девочек   Sh

es   여자에 대한 신사   Παρεκκλήσι για τα κορίτσια   Kuil untuk anak perempuan   Miếu thờ cho trẻ em gái   Santuario

вочек   Shrine for Girls   女の子のための神社   Schrein für Mädchen   Santuario de las niñas   מקדש עבור בנות   Храм за

Santuario per le ragazze   ضريح للفتيات   Scrín do chailíní   女孩的神殿   Svatyně pro dívky   लड़कियों के लिए तीर्थ   Sant

ам за момичета   Sanctuaire pour les filles   여자에 대한 신사   Παρεκκλήσι για τα κορίτσια   Kuil untuk anak peremp

Santuário para meninas   Храм для девочек   Shrine for Girls   女の子のための神社   Schrein für Mädchen   Santuario

k perempuan   Miếu thờ cho trẻ em gái   Santuario per le ragazze   ضريح للفتيات   Scrín do chailíní   女孩的神殿   Sva

ntuario de las niñas   מקדש עבור בנות   Храм за момичета   Sanctuaire pour les filles   여자에 대한 신사   Παρεκκλήσι γ

殿   Svatyně pro dívky   लड़कियों के लिए तीर्थ   Santuário para meninas   Храм для девочек   Shrine for Girls   女の子のた

ρεκκλήσι για τα κορίτσια   Kuil untuk anak perempuan   Miếu thờ cho trẻ em gái   Santuario per le ragazze   للفتيات

子のための神社   Schrein für Mädchen   Santuario de las niñas   מקדש עבור בנות   Храм за момичета   Sanctuaire pour

للفت   Scrín do chailíní   女孩的神殿   Svatyně pro dívky   लड़कियों के लिए तीर्थ   Santuário para meninas   Храм

ctuaire pour les filles   여자에 대한 신사   Παρεκκλήσι για τα κορίτσια   Kuil untuk anak perempuan   Miếu thờ cho trẻ

ninas   Храм для девочек   Shrine for Girls   女の子のための神社   Schrein für Mädchen   Santuario de las niñas   בנות

u thờ cho trẻ em gái   Santuario per le ragazze   للفتيات   Scrín do chailíní   女孩的神殿   Svatyně pro dívky   ל

as   מקדש עבור בנות   Храм за момичета   Sanctuaire pour les filles   여자에 대한 신사   Παρεκκλήσι για τα κορίτσια

dívky   लड़कियों के लिए तीर्थ   Santuário para meninas   Храм для девочек   Shrine for Girls   女の子のための神社   Schrein

κορίτσια   Kuil untuk anak perempuan   Miếu thờ cho trẻ em gái   Santuario per le ragazze   ضريح للفتيات   Scrín do ch

Schrein für Mädchen   Santuario de las niñas   מקדש עבור בנות   Храм за момичета   Sanctuaire pour les filles   여ㅈ

n do chailíní   女孩的神殿   Svatyně pro dívky   लड़कियों के लिए तीर्थ   Santuário para meninas   Храм для девочек   Shr

es   여자에 대한 신사   Παρεκκλήσι για τα κορίτσια   Kuil untuk anak perempuan   Miếu thờ cho trẻ em gái   Santuario